D1605453

KUBLAI KHAN

EMPEROR OF CHINA

THE MONGOLS™

KUBLAI KHAN

EMPEROR OF CHINA

ANDREW VIETZE

ROSEN

Published in 2017 by The Rosen Publishing Group, Inc.
29 East 21st Street, New York, NY 10010

Library of Congress Cataloging-in-Publication Data

Names: Vietze, Andrew
Title: Kublai Khan : emperor of China / Andrew Vietze.
Description: New York : Rosen Publishing, 2017. | Series: The Mongols. | Includes bibliographical references and index.
Identifiers: LCCN 2015050308 | ISBN 9781499463569 (library bound) | ISBN 9781499463545 (pbk.) | ISBN 9781499463552 (6-pack)
Subjects: LCSH: Kublai Khan, 1216-1294. | Mongols—Biography. | Mongols—History. | China—History—Yüan dynasty, 1260-1368. | China—Kings and rulers—Biography.
Classification: LCC DS752.6.K83 V54 2016 | DDC 951/.025092—dc23.

Manufactured in China

CONTENTS

INTRODUCTION...6

CHAPTER 1
A KHAN IS BORN...9

CHAPTER 2
KUBLAI KID...16

CHAPTER 3
AT WAR..25

CHAPTER 4
NEW KHAN ON THE BLOCK......................................31

CHAPTER 5
YUAN ANYONE?..37

CHAPTER 6
MARCO POLO...43

CHAPTER 7
EMPIRE FALLS...50

GLOSSARY...55

FOR MORE INFORMATION...57

FOR FURTHER READING...59

BIBLIOGRAPHY..60

INDEX...62

INTRODUCTION

When Marco Polo first visited China in 1275, the famed Italian merchant was astonished at what he found. Palaces of gold and silver. Public schools. Paper currency. Government censuses and secretaries. A postal service. Even bombs and gunpowder. The Far East land was far more developed than the Italian suspected—and in many ways far ahead of Europe. This was not a wilderness of barbarians or backward people, as many thought. The man who ruled over it all? The first non-Chinese emperor to rule all of China, a Mongol named Kublai Khan.

Marco Polo called Kublai Khan "lord of lords … the most powerful, in people, in lands, and in treasure, that is or ever was"—in other words, the most powerful ruler of all time. And the Italian traveler wasn't far off. Grandson of the feared Mongol warlord Genghis Khan, Kublai Khan inherited a vast empire—and then he doubled its size. His rule stretched from the Sea of Japan all the way across the Middle East to the borders of Europe. His subjects included almost half of the human population. For a time, Kublai Khan lorded over one-fifth of the earth's inhabited land area. His empire was the largest the world had known up to that point.

For all that, though, he is known less for conquering and more for spreading unity and culture. He wrote poetry, championed new ideas, and was a sponsor of the arts and learning. He set up programs to help the poor. He brought all of China together under one rule, unifying much of the

Stretching from the Pacific all the way to the Mediterranean, the Mongol Empire under Kublai Khan was the biggest the world had known up to that point.

Asian continent, and trade along the famous Silk Road was never better.

But it wasn't easy. Change never is. Kublai Khan's rise to power split the Mongols. Some loved him, but many did not, and he had to defeat his own brother to become the Great Khan. In many ways, he wasn't like other Mongols. They were a nomadic people, always moving and traveling, and he was famous for planting roots and ruling from a massive palace.

They tended to distrust people who weren't Mongol, and Kublai enjoyed meeting people from different cultures. Most Mongols were illiterate; Kublai was well educated. Mongols in the past had tended to kill their enemies and destroy their cultures, whereas Kublai let the Chinese live and learned as much as he could about their ways. Though he followed Mongol shamanist traditions, he even welcomed Chinese Confucian and Buddhist advisers to his administration. Other Mongols called him Setsen Khan or "Wise Khan."

Historians simply call him great. Kublai Khan is remembered as one of the most important rulers in history, a civilizing force that rose from a so-called barbaric people. He unified an entire continent of very different cultures—Chinese, Islamic, Russian, central Asian, Persian—spreading what historians called Pax Mongolica, or Mongolian Peace. And thanks to the stability of his rule and the sponsorship of his administration, the vast territory saw economic, social, and cultural advancements that were well ahead of much of the world. Some historians even give him credit for the discovery of America by Europeans. If he hadn't ruled China and impressed Marco Polo, European nations wouldn't have been so interested in finding a sea route to Asia in order to continue trading for silk and other Eastern products.

The world would have been a very different place if it weren't for one of its greatest leaders: Kublai Khan.

CHAPTER 1
A KHAN IS BORN

In 1213, Mongol warlord Genghis Khan drove his army through the Great Wall of China. The longest fortification in the world, the towering barrier was built by the Chinese to keep out the northern "barbarians"—tribes just like the Mongols. Genghis Khan passed through the wall easily, followed by his famous cavalry.

THE MONGOLS TAKE OVER CHINA

Under Genghis Khan, the Mongols had begun building an empire. From the vast plains of central Asia, they were expert horsemen, known for their skill with bow and arrow on horseback. This allowed them to attack with fearsome speed and mobility and enabled them to defeat almost everyone in their path. Genghis first united all the various tribes of Mongolia and then began to push outward. Many of the Mongols' enemies soon joined their ranks, growing their armies to massive proportions, and much of the medieval world feared them.

And now the great Mongol army had turned its attention to China. Genghis Khan spent years subduing the Jins, as the northern Chinese were known then. In June 1215, he was finally able to take their capital city, Zhongdu (today's Beijing). The Jins retreated south, giving the Mongols control of northern China.

Defeating the Jin army of northern China was an obsession of Kublai Khan's grandfather Genghis Khan. He finally did so around the time of Kublai's birth in 1215.

Expanding his rule into China had been a goal of Genghis Khan's for years. The son of a tribal chief, he began life in a tent in the semidesert of Mongolia. His father was poisoned by his enemies when Genghis was nine, and his family was expelled from their tribe. As a teenager he was even enslaved. But he learned and persevered, making a name for himself as a warrior and attracting followers. Now he reigned as khan, or great leader, over a growing empire. It stretched from the Pacific all the way to the edge of Europe in the west. He had wealth, many wives, and great power, and some say he was father to hundreds of children.

Kublai Khan is pictured here at about age forty-five, when he became Great Khan and established the Yuan dynasty.

And in September of 1215, he learned that his favorite son, Tolui, and remarkable daughter-in-law, Sorghaghtani, had given him another grandson.

It had been a good year for Genghis Khan.

At the time, he didn't know how important the taking of Zhongdu and the birth of his grandson would turn out to be. Those two moments in time would prove to be connected— and would change the course of history.

That boy was named Kublai.

KUBLAI'S REMARKABLE MOTHER

Historians know little about Kublai Khan's childhood because of his station in life. Though his father, Tolui, was one of Genghis Khan's favorites, he was the youngest, which meant he wasn't directly in line to succeed the Great Khan and was thus a relatively minor figure among the Mongols. He was still royalty but not given the status of his older brothers. Not the best or brightest of Genghis's royal children, Tolui became known as a military man and a drinker.

Tolui's wife, Sorghaghtani, however, was an entirely different story. Not a Mongol, she was a member of the Kerait tribe, a Turkish-speaking people. She was given to Tolui as a gift by Genghis, after the Mongols defeated the Keraits in 1200. By all accounts, Sorghaghtani was a remarkable woman—very intelligent, confident, capable, and ambitious. Because Tolui was often off on a campaign fighting with the Mongol army, she was the head of their household.

Genghis Khan and the Mongol Empire

Genghis Khan wasn't always Genghis or a khan. He began life as a boy named Temujin, the son of a tribal chief. The Mongol people were nomads, living a simple life of hunting and herding. They were largely illiterate and lived in small groups. Rival tribes would sometimes wage war on one another, but the Mongols didn't have too much interest in the wider world—until Genghis Khan. When he was barely out of his teens, he gathered warriors around himself. He was a master strategist and clever politician and made alliances among all the various tribes in Mongolia, uniting them as one. In 1206, he was proclaimed universal ruler, or Genghis Khan.

He undertook his first invasion in 1209, attacking the kingdom of Xia Xia, in northwestern China. He prevailed and proceeded to move east to take the kingdom of the Jins. After subduing the Jins, he moved against the Khwarazmian dynasty in what is now Iran. The ruler there, a shah, had sent Genghis Khan the heads of the men the Mongols had sent as envoys. After defeating the Khwarazmians, the Mongols took what is now Afghanistan, then much of Russia. The khan's men continued to amass victories, territory, and treasure. Present-day Armenia and Azerbaijan both fell.

When he died during a campaign against the Xias in 1227, Genghis Khan ruled over the largest empire the world had known to that point. The Mongols controlled everything from the eastern edge of China to beyond the Caspian Sea, into modern-day Turkey and Russia. Though history often remembers him as a conqueror, Genghis Khan was a smart

(continued on the next page)

(continued from the previous page)

politician. Rather than destroy and enslave, as the "barbarians" of the past would have done, he spared his subjects and learned from them. He allowed people to worship as they pleased. He refined government administration, setting up a code of laws. He built a system of couriers and a postal service so that he could communicate effectively with all of his faraway territories. He opened his empire to traders from outside.

Though he was known as a conqueror and warrior, Genghis Khan had established traditions of respect and religious and cultural tolerance. This was unusual, for any people, at this time. Sorghaghtani took these ideas even further. She

Kublai's mother, Sorghaghtani, ruled much of Mongolia when Kublai's father, Tolui, died, and she became famous in Asia for her intelligence, confidence, and wise rule.

was very aware that the Mongol Empire was huge and full of varied peoples. She also knew that, as royalty, her sons would one day play important roles in it so she made sure they were well versed in Genghis's famous code of laws and in Mongol traditions. But she also made sure they were familiar with the religions and traditions of the other peoples of the empire. She brought Chinese, Buddhist, and Confucian scholars into their home to educate Kublai. He had a series of tutors in Chinese, and he could write in the Mongol language. Surprisingly, he never learned to read Chinese, though he could read Mongol. Sorghaghtani also made sure that each of her boys became skilled horsemen and learned to use swords, spears, and bows.

A bright child, Kublai took to it all, and he enjoyed learning the ways of the warrior. He also liked to hunt, a passion that would stay with him throughout his life. Mongolia was an arid land of desert and plains, low hills and mountains, and Kublai loved the outdoors.

Taught by his gifted mother, surrounded by his brothers, Kublai grew smart and strong.

CHAPTER 2
KUBLAI KID

As Kublai grew, the Mongols continued to conquer, taking over more and more lands. The empire was shaken in 1227, when Genghis died. Kublai was just twelve. The Great Khan had picked Kublai's uncle Ogedei to succeed him as emperor, and his other sons, including Kublai's father, Tolui, each inherited a region to rule. As the youngest, Kublai's father received Genghis's "hearth land," their homeland of Mongolia. Tolui was very close to his brother Ogedei and had no plans to rival him, as some royal siblings did, and he devoted his time to helping the Mongols succeed militarily, taking off on campaigns to help subdue the remaining parts of China. Four years into one such action in northern China, Tolui tried to save his brother from a poisoning attempt and died.

SORGHAGHTANI'S RULE OF HEBEI PROVINCE

Tolui's death in 1232 left Kublai's mother largely in control of Mongolia. She had to report to Ogedei Khan for his final say on matters, but she could rule as she saw fit. The Great Khan gave her authority over her own army, legal matters, and the local population. "All should be under the control of her command," he ruled. Ogedei Khan then suggested Sorghaghtani marry his son, which would bind their families together. She politely declined, saying she had to look after her own sons.

Ogedei Khan gave Sorghaghtani the farmlands of Hebei Province to rule when Kublai was in his early twenties, and he learned much about governing from her.

Sorghaghtani was then in her forties and in one of the most powerful positions in the empire. Many sang her praises. Historian Rashid al-Din called her "extremely intelligent and able" and noted that the Great Khan often consulted her on affairs of state. A Hebrew visitor wrote, "All the princes marveled at her power of administration."

When Ogedei finally retook northern China, Sorghaghtani asked him for a piece. The Mongols had a tradition of giving out grants to family members when they conquered a land. And besides, Sorghaghtani pointed out, Ogedei owed it to her husband, who had died for him. She was given a section of Hebei Province, including the city of Zhengding, which likely had a population of about half a million people. Ogedei probably agreed to give this land to her because it wasn't the sort of place Mongols liked anyway. It was mostly agrarian, filled with peasant farmers. Because they were traditionally hunters and herders, Mongols didn't have much use for farmers or their sedentary life of staying in one place.

But Sorghaghtani saw the potential. Rather than continue age-old Mongol traditions of destruction and domination—conquering, enslaving, and heavily taxing the people—Sorghaghtani tried new ways of government. She borrowed ideas from Genghis, preaching tolerance. She realized that if she treated the locals well, encouraged them, and supported their farming efforts, she could yield great revenue in the form of taxes. She invited local scholars into the household to tutor her sons in Chinese ways. Her methods worked. Monies flowed in, and her subjects were largely happy and peaceful.

KUBLAI LEARNS HOW TO GOVERN

In his early twenties, Kublai watched his mother and uncle rule. His uncle had granted him lands, too, a region south of his mother's. He didn't have much interest in civic administration, and he simply let the local officials do what they'd always done. The results were disastrous, with widespread corruption and hardly any tax revenues. People from the area fled to Sorghaghtani's territory.

When Kublai Khan began to rule, he rewrote the harsh tax laws for which the Mongols were famous, and his legacy carried on for years after his death.

Kublai decided—or perhaps was told by his mother—to enact reforms. He set up a system similar to the one his mother used, rewrote the harsh tax laws, and helped the locals. Things began to change: families that had left returned, monies started to flow in, and Kublai learned valuable lessons about governance.

KUBLAI AND THE CHINESE

Kublai's mother made sure he learned from Chinese scholars as a boy. When he was older, Kublai sought out advisers and mentors from among the Chinese. When he was thirty years old, he befriended a prominent Buddhist monk named Haiyun, who provided valuable counsel to Kublai, then just a governor, and helped him understand the way the Chinese people thought. He told Kublai that Buddhism was the path to follow if he wanted to promote peace, relieve suffering, shun extravagance, and tell right from wrong. The pair were so close that Haiyun even named Kublai's second son.

Kublai would continue to surround himself with Chinese advisers, both Buddhists and Confucians, throughout his reign. He showed the Chinese great respect and adopted many of their ways. He sponsored the Chinese arts, and he built a famine relief program to help the poor. He followed Chinese governmental practices, continuing their civil service and appointing Chinese bureaucrats. He gave his empire a Chinese name, the Yuan dynasty. He would eventually move his capital from Mongolia to the site of today's Beijing. Even the Chinese warlords admired him.

POLITICAL MANEUVERING

While Kublai was learning how to lead, a game of thrones began for control of the empire. Off on a hunting party in December 1241, Kublai's uncle Odegei, the Great Khan, suddenly died, and his death left behind a power vacuum that several rushed forward to fill. The two main candidates were Kublai's cousin Guyuk, Ogedei's oldest son, and another of Kublai's cousins, Batu. Batu led the Golden Horde, the Mongol clan that inhabited southern Russia. Guyuk was originally the successor chosen by the Great Khan himself, and he and Batu disliked each other. Ogedei grew annoyed with his son's behavior toward his older cousin and selected a grandson to rule instead, leaving a confusing mess behind when he died suddenly.

A *kurultai* was called. This was a meeting of the royal families at which a vote was taken and a new leader anointed. Guyuk won and was appointed khan. His mother, Kublai's aunt, had worked tirelessly to see him crowned. Sorghaghtani, meanwhile, did something similar behind the scenes: she forged covert alliances with royal families that would one day benefit her sons.

Kublai's mother's efforts paid off when Guyuk decided to attack Batu. Though he was Great Khan, Guyuk wanted to get rid of his enemy and any further challenge to the throne. Sorghaghtani heard of the khan's plan ahead of time and

Kublai's older brother Mongke became the fourth Great Khan in 1251, thanks to the covert alliances made by their mother, Sorghaghtani.

secretly warned Batu. It was a big risk, for if the khan discovered she'd plotted against him, he would execute her and her entire family. If it paid off, however, the line of succession to the emperor could switch to her family. Batu had given up on becoming khan and had turned his attention back toward Russia. Kublai's brother Mongke was the next logical choice.

Sorghaghtani's decision worked beautifully. Guyuk Khan died en route to the battle of causes history has forgotten. Batu decided to throw his support behind Mongke, but a lot of other Mongols from Ogedei's line disagreed, and they put together the first violent opposition since the death of Genghis. Many were killed in the battles that followed. Kublai's older brother emerged victorious as Great Khan in 1251 when Kublai was thirty-six.

KUBLAI'S NEW RESPONSIBILITIES

Two years later, Kublai asked his brother Mongke Khan for more responsibility in the empire. He wanted a larger piece of northern China to govern. Mongke granted his wish and gave him a large territory along the Wei River and the border with the Song dynasty of the south. It was another pastoral area made up of farms and farmers, and Kublai had a clever idea. He set up "military farms," which generated food specifically for the army, and Mongke was very pleased. Kublai also ruled using the precepts he learned from his mother and following the advice he learned from his Chinese advisers. He set up a pacification bureau, to keep the peace, and even a bank to print paper money. He governed with great success, and the Mongols took notice.

In 1252, his brother Mongke gave Kublai a new challenge. He was to subdue the Dali people to his south, in order to give the Mongols a base from which to invade the powerful Song dynasty of southern China. It was a daunting task. The Dalis lived in a mountainous region of thick jungle that was not easy for the Mongols' famous cavalry to move through.

If he were successful, though, the Mongols would one day rule all of China.

CHAPTER 3
AT WAR

Though he had experience fighting in battle, Kublai Khan had never led men into combat. He had never before had the opportunity to direct the mighty Mongols at what history said they did best—conquering. He was now thirty-seven, but he'd always played a secondary role to his uncles or brothers. His brother Mongke made sure that Kublai had some help, sending along one of his best generals, the son of the legendary general Subutai, who had subdued half of Asia with Genghis Khan.

KUBLAI'S FIRST COMBAT OPERATION

The attack on the land of the Dali people—today's Yunnan Province—was a very strategic move on the part of Mongke Khan. If they succeeded at taking the territory, the Mongols would have a straight shot at the Song dynasty through its weak western border, and Mongke wanted two fronts on which to attack the Song. The Dali route would give him just what he needed.

He also knew that this Tibetan/Burmese tribe had very little in the way of an army. The terrain would be a challenge, though. The region where the Dali lived was defined by skyscraping mountains, a massive lake, and the mighty Yangtze River. The Mongols would have to squeeze their

FIGHTING LIKE A MONGOL

What made the Mongols such fearsome warriors? How could a relatively small tribe from central Asia, wearing sheepskins and leather, defeat armies of heavily armored knights and conquer almost half of the inhabited world?

In 1241, German emperor Frederick II appealed to other Europeans seeking help against the Mongols. "They wear raw hides of oxen and to these are sewn iron plates," he wrote. "They are incomparable archers. The bow is a more familiar weapon to them than to any other people ... they have entirely subdued other nations because of this." Where the Germans and other Europeans were slowed by heavy plate armor, rode huge armored war-horses, and needed to get in close to fight with swords, maces, and other hand weapons, the Mongols were fast and mobile. Expert horsemen, they were able to literally ride circles around their opponents, and they were very adept at using bows while mounted. With them, the Mongols could attack with lightning speed and deliver killing blows to their enemies.

They were also extremely well organized, divided into regiments of warriors, first by tens, then by hundreds, and on up into the thousands. Leaders of each group could be given different instructions, allowing for complex maneuvers. Unlike other cultures, the Mongols expected all men of a certain age to have armor and weapons and be skilled fighters, not just the nobility, as was the case in Japan and Europe. And finally, they used psychological warfare, too, firing huge masses of howling arrows that would scream through the sky and terrify their opponents. All together, these tactics made the Mongols into some of history's greatest warriors.

army between them, which would give the Dali opportunities for ambush and a very defensible position.

Kublai tried diplomacy first, sending three ambassadors to try to persuade the Dali to surrender without a fight, but his men were all executed.

KUBLAI OUTWITS HIS ENEMIES

The army led by Kublai met the Dali at China's famous Yang-tze River. Kublai's army was to the west, the Dali to the east. The Dali were confident that the river—third-longest in the world after the Nile and the Amazon—would stop the Mongols from advancing, at least at that point. Kublai decided to use a trick that Genghis had once used to cross the Yellow River and surprise his enemy. The Mongols made rafts out of sheepskin and mobilized at night, while the Dali were sleeping. Crossing silently, they attacked at dawn—on unsuspecting prey—and routed the Dali, forcing them to retreat.

The Dali were completely overrun, and the Mongols could have run riot on their capital city, also called Dali, enacting revenge for the killing of their ambassadors. But under Kublai's orders, they didn't, instead sparing the city. Kublai allowed the ruling family to remain in place alongside one of his appointed governors, and their laws were left largely intact. He even gave city residents oxen and seeds to help with their next harvest.

His brother, the Great Khan, could only be happy with Kublai's first venture as a military leader—he defeated his

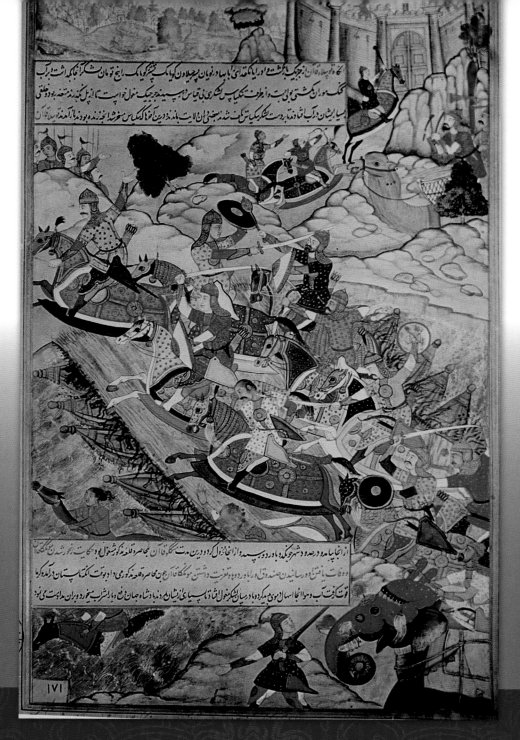

Though known as horsemen, the Mongols occasionally took to the water. Kublai cleverly made use of a pontoon bridge to cross the Yangtze River and catch the Dali by surprise.

enemy, took very few casualties, and added a very strategic territory to the Mongol Empire. Not only was it ideal for an invasion of the Song dynasty, but it also opened up new trade opportunities with India and Burma.

And it set the stage for Kublai's rise as a Mongol leader.

KUBLAI'S POWER GROWS

After the success of his campaign against the Dali, Kublai returned to govern the territory his brother had given him. Perhaps due to his accomplishments, it was now larger. Mongke

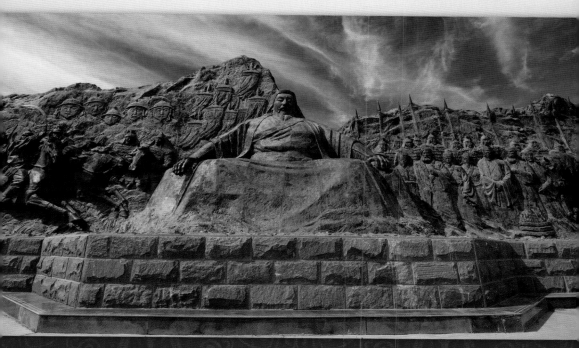

Xanadu, the new capital Kublai Khan had constructed for himself, was in many ways finer than the palace of the Great Khan in Mongolia. Today, the word "Xanadu" is used to describe an idyllic place of wonder, serenity, and great beauty.

had added more lands to Kublai's administration, and Kublai was now responsible for much of China. He continued to govern as he had learned from Genghis and his mother, and he developed close relationships with many Chinese. He had several trusted Chinese advisers, and with their help he set up a new city for his domain on the steppes in Chinese territory, called Shangdu (or, as Westerners called it, Xanadu), basing its design on Chinese capitals of the past. He started up public schools to ready his subjects for contributions to the empire, and he also sponsored Chinese cultural events. In many ways, Kublai's palace at Xanadu was finer than the Great Khan's in Karakorum, the Mongol capital.

All of these actions began to arouse suspicion among Kublai's fellow Mongols. Many thought he was becoming too much like his "sedentary" subjects—too Chinese. It was an accusation that would plague him his entire career.

And Kublai had further problems. Mongke had sent him to battle the Song, the remaining Chinese powers. While on this campaign, a secret messenger brought word that Mongke had died after ten days of illness while beginning the great invasion of the Song dynasty. Some historians believe he carried an injury from an earlier battle, while others think he contracted cholera or dysentery from contaminated water. Kublai knew the news would disturb his troops, so he kept it quiet.

He also knew it would leave another power vacuum in the Mongol world—one that he himself was destined to fill.

CHAPTER 4
NEW KHAN ON THE BLOCK

The plan had been for the Mongols to attack in a trident, with Mongke leading a force against Sichuan. Kublai's troops were to march south from Xanadu, covering more than 800 miles (1,287 kilometers); Kublai himself was initially told to stay home. He was fighting gout, an ailment that would bother him for the remainder of his life. He didn't want to be left out of the fight, however, and implored his brother to send him. Mongke allowed it, and Kublai rode at the head of a massive army of Mongols.

He covered more than 600 miles (966 km) and was about to engage with a Song troop when he heard about the khan's death. The typical thing to do in this situation would be to retreat, begin the burial arrangements, and arrange for a new kurultai. The process would take months, though, and Kublai was concerned that the Song would become stronger during the delay. And he also must have thought that defeating the Song, which no Mongols had been able to do before, would put him in a very strong position when the next kurultai was called.

SHOULD I STAY OR SHOULD I GO?

Kublai decided the better course would be to attack. According to historian Rashad al-Din, he dismissed the talk of Mongke's death as a rumor designed to weaken his troops, and he continued his invasion, dispatching the Song troops in front of him. Then he made the difficult crossing of the Yangtze River and moved on the Song forces at Wuchang. The Mongols had the upper hand until Song reinforcements returned from Sichuan, where they had been battling Mongke's troops until he died. The fight turned into a stalemate that lasted a couple of months.

Kublai faced a difficult choice: stay in Wuchang and try to break the Song once and for all, or return home, where succession plans were surely being made. Then he was visited by another secret courier with word that his younger brother Ariq was assembling an army back home in Mongolia. It could be for only one thing: to seize power. Kublai decided to return to Mongolia.

SIBLING RIVALRY

Kublai's brother Ariq was far more traditional than Kublai or even their other brother Hulegu, who had become ruler of Persia (the Il-Khanate). While Kublai and Hulegu were open to new cultures and customs, Ariq was a staunchly traditional Mongol who believed Mongol ways were best. He didn't approve of Kublai and Hulegu's "sedentary" ways; he thought that Mongols shouldn't live in and adopt the practices of the peoples they conquered. Ariq gathered other conservative Mongols around him, held a false kurultai, and proclaimed himself khan.

Kublai, of course, was irate. Various princes from the empire rallied around him in China and urged him to hold a quick kurultai and take the mantle of khan. Though it was the first

KUBLAI'S FAMILY TREE

Kublai was not the only Great Khan in the family. His grandfather was Genghis Khan, the great warlord who built the Mongol empire. His uncle Ogedei and cousin Guyuk were both Great Khan before an alliance forged by Sorghaghtani switched the line of rule to the Tolui family. Then Kublai's brothers Mongke and Ariq both became khan, in Ariq's case only briefly. Kublai's younger brother Hulegu became the ruler of the Persian Empire (Il-Khanate). After Kublai's death in 1294, his grandson Temur became Great Khan.

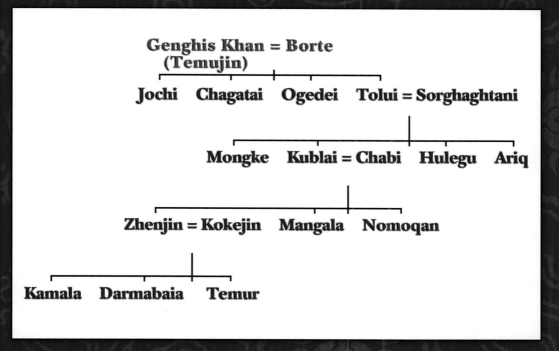

Kublai Khan's family was a "who's who" of Asian rulers. His grandfather was the world-famous Genghis Khan, and his mother gave birth to four emperors.

time a khan had ascended to the throne in a foreign land, which made it contestable, in May 1260, at the age of forty-five, Kublai Khan did just that.

BROTHER VERSUS BROTHER

Two men obviously couldn't rule at the same time, and the empire was suddenly divided. Kublai returned to his palace in China and sent out a proclamation, aligning himself with the

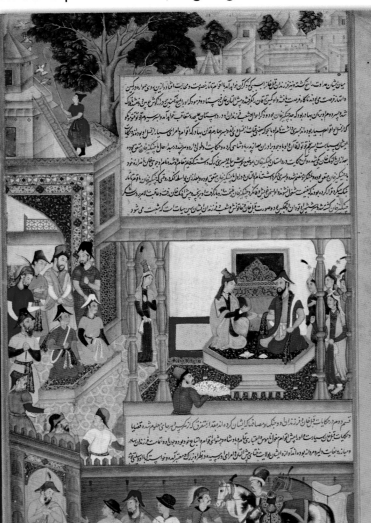

In 1260, forty-five-year-old Kublai Khan was proclaimed Great Khan in a ceremony at his palace in China.

Chinese emperors of the past. While the Mongols were superior warriors, he wrote, the Chinese were better at forming governments and ruling. A wise leader was needed to unify the empire and check the rebelliousness of Ariq and his men. Kublai put himself forward as the answer and pointed out that he had been a good ruler and helped the masses. He also promised to reduce taxes and make sure the poor were fed. He ended his proclamation by encouraging civilians and military personnel to support him for the good of the empire.

The Chinese responded to Kublai's appeal, and many in the north supported him. Ariq may have had a few more supporters among Mongol royalty, but Kublai had the people behind him—and, more importantly, he had control of far more territory. This would turn out to be his greatest weapon against his brother. Ariq's hostility to the "sedentary" life left him with few resources for food and arms production. Kublai controlled vast agricultural resources, supplying his armies and people with food, and he strategically cut off access to all the areas he didn't control so that his brother couldn't get to them. Ariq was limited to Karakorum and Siberia to the north, which didn't produce enough food to support his troops.

CIVIL WAR

Bloodshed was inevitable. Kublai's armies advanced on Karakorum, forcing Ariq to pull back, and Kublai's allies defeated the forces loyal to Ariq in China. Many Mongols on both sides were killed, and Ariq survived by making alliances with leaders in central Asia, who for a time were able to supply him with resources. Kublai's men took the upper hand, driving Ariq north into Siberia and cutting off even more of his support. Ariq's allies began to turn away from him, or they were executed by Kublai. All looked bleak for Kublai's little brother.

In 1264, Ariq recognized he was defeated and came to his brother in submission. The pair had a meeting in Kublai's "tent palace" and tearfully made up. Kublai struggled with what to do with his brother. Ultimately he spared his life but kept him under arrest. Most of Ariq's chief lieutenants were executed. One, however, declared his new devotion to Kublai by saying, "Today Kublai Kahn is ruler of the face of the earth."

The bloody Toluid Civil War lasted four years and almost tore the Mongol Empire apart.

CHAPTER 5
YUAN ANYONE?

The Mongol civil war was finally over. An ugly, bloody affair, it had weakened the Mongols, given strength to their enemies, and caused a lot of pain and suffering. Two years after their reconciliation, Kublai's brother Ariq died. Shortly thereafter, the other three potential threats for the throne of the Mongols—Hulegu, Kublai's other brother and Persian king; Berke, who succeeded his brother Batu as leader of the Golden Horde; and Alghu, who ruled Chagatei's lands—all died, too. Kublai was at the top all by himself. He was almost fifty years old and in complete control.

Around this time, Kublai made a bold decision that showed just how secure he felt as the leader of the Mongols. He moved his capital to today's Beijing, the city his grandfather Genghis had conquered the year he was born. It was a significant step in that it took his base deeper into China than his palace at Xanadu—and thus farther from Mongolia. And he would never have done so if he felt threatened by the conservative Mongols, who always accused him of becoming too Chinese.

BIRTH OF A DYNASTY

The old Jin capital was largely in ruin after decades of fighting, but Kublai found a section to the north and west of the city that was beautiful. On an island in a lake, he had his temporary

In the late 1260s Kublai Khan built a new imperial city, Dadu, on the site of today's Beijing, moving his rule further into the heart of China.

palace built, and then construction of the new Imperial City, called Dadu, began. It took more than a decade, but the new capital began to take shape, and it was a marvel to behold, full of ramparts, gilded palaces, majestic courtyards, and a central hall that could seat six thousand guests. Visitors were completely overwhelmed and in awe of the place. It's said that Kublai had grass from the steppes of Mongolia planted outside his palace so he'd never forget his roots.

The Great Khan wanted a showplace befitting the emperor who ruled by heaven's mandate—that was how the Chinese viewed their leaders and how he wanted to be seen. And he felt that the spectacular new capital deserved to be the capital of all of China, the beginning of a whole new dynasty in Chinese history. He and his Chinese advisers came up with a fitting name for this new dynasty—Yuan—which meant "first," "fundamental," or "principal."

The Yuan dynasty was given its official unveiling in December 1271. The Chinese had long thought of their governments as dynasties, and establishing a new one signified to Kublai's Chinese subjects that the emperor took them and their culture seriously.

ATTACKING THE SONG

Kublai had most of the things he had ever wanted—wives, a family, control of the empire, beautiful palaces, the respect of most of his people. Only one thing was missing—a unified China. Ever since Genghis Khan had battled the Song, the Mongols had wanted the southern Chinese lands. Unlike the grasslands and desert to the north, the south of China was a rich land of lakes and rivers, exquisite farmland, and cities on the sea. The Song were also very prosperous, trading as far away as India and the Middle East. Kublai probably coveted this terrain more than anyone before him; he wanted all of China, one great nation under him, and there was only one way he was going to get it. The Song refused to submit.

The major strength of the Song was their navy—their army was no match for the Mongols—and to defeat them would take an impressive fleet of well-trained sailors. But what did horsemen from the grasslands know about boats? Kublai would learn, using his vast resources to build a navy. He had boat builders working around the clock to construct enough ships to match the Song.

The attack began in 1267 with the siege of Xiangyang, a very strategically important border city at the meeting place of several important rivers. For five years, the Mongols battered the city; it was one of the longest sieges in medieval history. They built a blockade to try to strangle supply routes, starving the occupants. But supplies somehow kept sneaking in, and the Mongols and Song were at a stalemate militarily.

WAR MACHINES

Kublai remembered his brother Hulegu telling him about the massive siege engines that the Persians had used to take Baghdad, and he called in the two engineers who had designed them. Unlike the small, man-powered Mongol trebuchet, these tall towers used counterweights to throw rocks big enough to take down walls.

The khan had two 60-foot (18-meter) trebuchets built and used them to take Xiangyang's smaller sister city, Fancheng. They proved devastatingly effective. Fancheng's dead were piled high in full view of Xiangyang, and then the catapult was turned on Xiangyang and fired a single 220-pound (100-kilogram) shot against one of the city's skyscraping guard towers. As a Mongol general recalled: "The noise shook the city like

To break the stalemate he'd reached against his enemies the Song, Kublai Khan ordered construction of two trebuchet siege engines capable of hurling stones big enough to destroy fortress walls.

a clap of thunder, and everything inside the city was in utter confusion." It wasn't long before the leaders of Xiangyang decided to surrender to avoid a fate similar to Fancheng's.

THE SONG DYNASTY CRUMBLES

The fall of Xiangyang in 1273 was felt like a shockwave through the Song dynasty. Cities to the south felt very vulnerable, and the Mongols advanced right through southern China's heartland. Then the Song emperor died with little forewarning, which demoralized the Song even further. And it wasn't long before the Mongols fell upon the Song capital,

LIFE UNDER KUBLAI

Kublai Khan spared the city of Xiangyang and its residents. Life was to continue on normally for the people of the Song. Compared to other conquerors, Kublai Khan treated the Chinese with great respect. He would even use public funds to help widows, children, and the poor. Officials were replaced by Mongols, but otherwise everything was largely as it had been before. The Great Khan knew that to keep the people happy, they had to have their needs met, and to feed them, he'd have to keep the farmers on his side. He instituted reforms among peasant farmers, building great grain warehouses. And, in a symbolic move, he no longer allowed Mongols to graze their herds on farmland. He built schools in rural areas and improved irrigation.

Peace and harmony among his subjects was important to the Great Khan. He believed that it showed he truly ruled with a mandate from heaven, and he also thought that if he were worthy of this mandate, he was worthy of fulfilling his grandfather's mission: to eventually rule the world.

Hangzhou.

The Mongols surrounded the city and choked its supply lines for years. The emperor's widow was at first defiant, but in January 1276, she sent word of her capitulation. "I respectfully bow a hundred times to Your Majesty," she wrote, "the Benevolent, Brilliant, Spiritual, and Martial Emperor of the Great Yuan."

CHAPTER 6
MARCO POLO

Kublai Khan did it—he was able to accomplish what none of his predecessors could, not his brothers, not his father, not even his world-famous grandfather, Genghis Khan. He'd defeated the Song dynasty and united China, the first non-Chinese leader to do so. His empire now stretched from the South China Sea across Asia to Europe—the largest empire that the world had ever known. He had palaces and riches and power beyond compare.

This was the world that Italian merchant Marco Polo stepped into with his father, Nicolo, and uncle, Maffeo. Traveling merchants, the two older Polos were working in Bukhara (today's Uzbekistan) when they were approached by an envoy from Kublai Khan's court and asked if they would pay the Great Khan a visit. He'd never met a European before and had many questions. The Polos agreed and in 1266 were ushered in to meet the Great Khan. He queried them about European government, law, and religious traditions, and he asked if they would deliver a note to the pope for him. Kublai wanted one hundred Christians to come to China to share what they knew of the arts, music, science, mathematics, and religion. He gave the Polos a foot-long gold tablet that marked them as his emissaries and assured their safe passage, and then he sent them back to Italy.

Born in Venice in 1254, Marco was already a teen and had never met his father until Nicolo returned from Kublai's court.

In 1271, Kublai made an important new friend, a young Italian merchant named Marco Polo (kneeling, in green, with his father and uncle), whose journals would make Kublai famous throughout the world.

Marco had been raised in one of the great cities of the Mediterranean and was brought up as a young gentleman, well educated and well mannered. When he was seventeen, the three Polos set out on the long return trip to the Far East—a journey of more than 5,000 miles (8,047 km)—bearing letters and gifts from the pope. For much of the way, they traveled the fabled Silk Road, the ancient trade route that linked the Middle East and China. Full of sandstorms, bandits, brutal desert conditions, and death, the trip took the Polos more than three years, but finally, in 1275, they arrived.

MARCO POLO AND KUBLAI

Marco Polo became a trusted friend, confidant, and courier for Kublai Khan. He knew

THE SILK ROAD

Though it's called the Silk Road, this famous trade "highway" was not actually a single road—and a lot more flowed across it than silks. The Silk Road was actually a series of trade routes that linked the East and West as far back as 130 BCE, when the Han dynasty opened China to foreign trade, and some historians think it wiser to call them the Silk Routes. Usually starting at Damascus or some other port on the Mediterranean, these overland passages took merchants from the bazaars of Syria across the Arabian deserts to India and China. Merchants from the West traded for spices, silk, gold, and other items. But it wasn't only goods that were exchanged—the Silk Road took travelers from one culture to another, exposing peoples to different religions, governments and politics, languages, arts, science, and military strategies. The Silk Road is credited with much development of Asia and the Middle East.

Marco Polo was amazed at many of the things he saw in Kublai Khan's China, like paper money, the use of credit, the printing of books, coal burning, firearms, and the Yuan dynasty's sophisticated postal service.

at least four languages, making him a valuable translator. He traveled widely to India and Burma, bringing messages from the khan, and some of the places he went wouldn't see another Westerner for centuries. He was full of amazement from the moment he stepped into Kublai's palace, describing the riches and wonders with a keen eye for detail. Even the smallest things impressed him, such as coal. He had never seen "stones that burned like logs," and he thought they were remarkably efficient. He was also impressed that the Chinese used paper money to buy goods, unheard of in Europe at the time. "With these pieces of paper," he gushed, "they can buy anything and pay for anything."

Marco Polo was amazed by the sophisticated canal system that allowed for both public transportation and irrigation, and he marveled at the printing of books, the use of credit, and the massive Chinese economy, which far outpaced Europe in many ways. He was especially taken with the khan's imperial message service, which was unlike anything he'd ever seen and allowed Kublai to communicate with the farthest reaches of his empire.

THE FRIENDS PART WAYS

After more than seventeen years in China, the Polos became homesick for their native Italy. Marco Polo approached Kublai Khan, telling his friend it was time for them to go home. The Great Khan refused to let him leave—he valued their friendship

THE TRAVELS OF MARCO POLO

Published around 1300, The Travels of Marco Polo *was one of the biggest books of its time.*

Even though *The Travels of Marco Polo* bears his name, Marco Polo didn't actually write the book that introduced Kublai Khan to Europe. He told the tale to writer Rustichello while they were both prisoners of war during the conflict between the Italian republics of Genoa and Venice in 1298. And Rustichello had the good sense to write it all down.

It's a remarkable document, chronicling the twenty-four years Polo explored China, but historians question whether it's all true. Polo seemed to claim, for example, that he was at the siege of Xiangyang—but he didn't arrive in China until two years after the Song city had fallen. This led some to debate whether Polo ever even made it to China at all. Some critics point out that he never mentioned everyday Chinese items like chopsticks or the common practice of foot binding, which were very unusual to Europeans, and claim he picked up all these stories from travelers in Persia. But other details are so strong that historians now generally believe that he did indeed visit Kublai Khan and that most of the tales are true, but he either made up some material or it was changed in translation when Rustichello wrote it all down. Other Europeans had visited the Far East before, and Chinese and Persian writers had written about Kublai Khan, but Marco Polo brought a richness to the story of the Great Khan that would have been lost to history without him.

too much to allow it. Marco Polo figured out a way around this difficulty in 1291, agreeing to escort the Mongol princess Kokachin to Persia, where she would marry Kublai Khan's great-nephew, the Il-Khan of Persia.

Marco Polo's stories resonated throughout Europe. The romance and riches of the Far East were very appealing to many Europeans, including his own countrymen. There was one in particular who was so inspired by the tales of the Venetian that he set off to find the sea route to Asia, bringing along with him a copy of Marco Polo's book. His name? Christopher Columbus.

Chapter 7
Empire Falls

In 1281, Kublai Khan suffered a great setback when his favorite wife, Chabi, died. They'd been together for more than forty years, and she'd been his most faithful companion—and one of his most trusted advisers. Kublai and Chabi had built a large family, including five daughters and four sons, and they'd been through all the successes and disappointments of his reign together. Despite their great wealth, she was always frugal and filled with common sense. She told him after he'd conquered the Song not to become too headstrong: "Your handmaiden has heard that from ancient times there has never been a kingdom that lasted a thousand years."

Kublai was crushed when she died. And more sorrow was to follow. Four years later, his favorite son—and his appointed successor—Zhenjin also died. Given the name True Gold by Kublai's friend and adviser Haiyun, Zhenjin was his father's pride and joy. For decades Kublai had been grooming Zhenjin to take his place as Great Khan, making sure he was well educated in Chinese history and culture, Buddhism, and, of course, the Mongol way. He was given his first region to rule at the age of twenty, and at the same time, he was appointed supervisor of the Privy Council, a very important role. Ten years later, he was proclaimed the heir apparent.

JAPANESE INVASIONS

Perhaps to show his importance, perhaps to fulfill the Mandate of Heaven, Kublai decided it was time to extend his power outward and take Japan. He'd given the emperor of Japan a warning in 1266, addressing him as the "ruler of a small country," and demanding that he pay tribute to the Great Khan. When he refused, Kublai Khan sent an invasion force of twenty-three thousand to attack the Japanese. During the attack, a typhoon hit, sending a third of Kublai's ships and about thirteen thousand men to the bottom of the sea. When they attacked again years later, on August 15, 1281, another typhoon hit the Yuan fleet. The winds and waves were brutal—the Japanese called them kamikaze, or "divine winds"—and they wasted no time destroying the Mongol navy. Only a few hundred ships survived.

(continued on the next page)

Kublai Khan's disastrous invasions of Japan in the 1270s and 1280s were among several setbacks that led to the emperor's decline.

(continued from the previous page)

Kublai Khan believed that Japan must be protected by super-natural forces, but he was still gravely disappointed. Japan would be added to a list of nations he was unable to conquer, including Korean holdouts, Indonesia, and Vietnam.

According to historians, these deaths set the Great Khan into a terrible depression. He began to overeat and grew obese, and he also began to drink heavily, both of which seriously affected his health. As his health declined and his weight grew, he suffered greatly from the gout that had bothered him much of his adult life. He tried to get help from doctors, medications, even from shamans and holy men, but nothing seemed to give him peace.

END OF AN ERA

Internally, his empire had begun to crumble, too. The Chagatei Khanate, which ruled under him in central Asia, began to rebel, as did the Golden Horde in Russia. And in parts of China, such as Manchuria, there was swelling dis-sent against him.

The Great Khan became despondent, and despite all he'd accomplished across his seven decades of life, he was plagued by self-doubt. He felt he failed in his mandate to continue Genghis's wish to demonstrate Mongol supremacy to the known world. Even his closest friends were unable to cheer him up.

With the death of his family members, the failed invasions, and internal strife all weighing on him, the depressed Kublai Khan died in the great hall of his palace at the age of eighty on February 18, 1294. He was taken to Burkhan Khaldun, in the Khenti Mountains, east of the Mongol capital, and laid to rest in a modest grave near his grandfather. The exact site of his burial remains a mystery to this day.

A LASTING LEGACY

Within a relatively short time after Kublai Kahn's death, much of the Mongol Empire crumbled away. In each corner, ethnic peoples rallied against them. Kublai's successor, his grandson Temur, held power for only twenty years, and within a century the Yuan dynasty had fallen.

But Kublai's legacy can still be seen in today's China. Each successive dynasty to follow the Yuan kept to largely the same bounds that Kublai created. In other words, they didn't want to give up the territory, including places such as Tibet and parts of Manchuria and Yunnan Province that were not traditionally Chinese lands.

Kublai Khan was unique among the Mongols in that he wanted not only to conquer but also to govern in the best way possible. He looked after the welfare of his subjects in a manner unheard of at the time, expanding schools and using social programs and public funds to take care of the poorest among them. His adoption and refinement of certain bureaucratic traditions in civil service and communications can still be seen today. In fact, many historians credit Genghis and Kublai Khan for beginning the modernization of the world. Centuries after Marco Polo, the famous British poet Samuel Taylor Coleridge further immortalized the Great Khan and his city of Shangdu, or Xanadu, in the famous poem "Kubla Khan."

Not a bad legacy for a guy who grew up in a tent on the steppes of Mongolia.

GLOSSARY

barbarian A member of a tribe thought to be uncivilized, primitive, and savage.

Buddhism A peaceful religion, sometimes called a philosophy because it has no god, practiced in much of Asia. Among its major ideas are a commitment to nonviolence and a belief in karma and reincarnation.

Chagatei Khanate A territory of the Mongol Empire in central Asia led by descendants of Genghis Khan's son Chagatei but still subject to the rule of the Great Khan.

Confucianism A philosophy or way of thinking derived from the ideas of the great Chinese thinker Confucius.

Dali People who lived in southwestern China (Yunnan Province).

Golden Horde The westernmost region of the Mongol Empire, near Russia; though it had its own khan and capital, it was still under the rule of the Great Khan.

Il-Khanate Led by Kublai Khan's brother Hulegu, this was the part of the Mongol Empire in Persia.

Jin People who lived in northern China, also sometimes called the Jurchen and known for the Jin dynasty (1115–1234).

Kerait A tribe of Turkish-speaking people that lived in central Asia near the Mongols.

khan A leader of the Mongols and other Asian peoples, first used to describe tribal chieftains, then rulers of territories, and finally the Great Khan.

kurultai A meeting at which the royal families of Mongolia determined the next khan.

Mandate of Heaven An ancient Chinese idea that rulers are granted the right to rule by heaven as long as they do so fairly and honorably.

nomadic Always on the move, like the tribal Mongols, who hunted and followed herds, pulling their tents and household items behind them.

sedentary Unmoving, stationary. This is how the nomadic Mongols saw many of their enemies, particularly those who farmed.

Shamanism A spiritual path that follows shamans, men or women who perceive and interpret signs from the spirit world.

Silk Road Name given to trade routes between China and the Middle East over which goods like silks and gold and spices traveled.

Song People of southeastern China, often divided into Northern and Southern Song, and known for the Song dynasty (960–1279).

steppe A largely flat treeless area of grasslands, especially in central Asia.

trebuchet A type of catapult that uses counterforces to swing an arm to throw missiles.

typhoon A tropical cyclone, also known as "divine wind" to the Japanese.

Xanadu Also known as Shangdu, Kublai Khan's first capital in China and later his "summer" capital, known for its peace and natural beauty.

Yuan dynasty The name Kublai Khan gave to his empire after unifying China. It remained in power from 1271 until 1368.

FOR MORE INFORMATION

Aga Khan Museum
77 Wynford Drive
Toronto, ON M3C 1K1
Canada
(416) 646-4677
Website: http://www.agakhanmuseum.org
Opened in 2014, the Aga Khan Museum is largely about Islamic
    culture, but it also offers a look at the cultures that lived at the
    western edge of the Mongol Empire.

Discover Mongolia
#1101, Metro Business Center, Baga toiruu, 6th khoroo
Sukhbaatar District
Ulaanbaatar
Mongolia
Website: http://www.discovermongolia.mn
Though largely tourism based, Discover Mongolia offers a wealth of
    information about the history, culture, and museums in Mongolia.

Marco Polo Museum
33, Plokata Square
Korcula Town, Korcula Island 20260
Croatia
Website: http://marcopolo.com.hr
Korcula, Croatia, is a town obsessed with Marco Polo, and this
    museum is a great resource of information on the explorer. It fea-
    tures a life-size exhibit of Marco Polo at Kublai Khan's court and
    has great image galleries online.

National Geographic
1145 17th Street NW
Washington, DC 20036
(800) 647-5463
Website: http://www.nationalgeographic.com
One of the oldest and largest scientific and educational organiza-
   tions in the world, National Geographic is home to a wealth of
   information about Mongolia, China, and the rest of Asia.

Smithsonian Institution
P.O. Box 37012
SI Building, Room 153, MRC 010
Washington, DC 20013-7012
(202) 633-1000
Website: http://www.si.edu
The largest museum/research complex in the world, the
   Smithsonian has hosted large-scale exhibits about the Mongols
   and done many features in its magazine on them as well.

WEBSITES

Because of the changing nature of Internet links, Rosen Publishing has developed an online list of websites related to the subject
of this book. This site is updated regularly. Please use this link to
access this list:

http://www.rosenlinks.com/MON/kublai

FOR FURTHER READING

Bergreen, Laurence. *Marco Polo: From Venice to Xanadu*. New York, NY: Random House, 2007.

Cotterell, Arthur, and Laura Buller. *DK Eyewitness Books: Ancient China*. New York, NY: Dorling Kindersley, 2005.

Ebrey, Patricia Buckley. *Cambridge Illustrated History of China*. New York, NY: Cambridge University Press, 2010.

Goldberg, Enid, and Norman Itzkowitz. *Genghis Khan: 13th Century Mongolian Tyrant*. New York, NY: Scholastic, 2009.

Herbert, Janis. *Marco Polo for Kids: His Marvelous Journey to China*. Chicago, IL: Chicago Review Press, 2001.

Krull, Kathleen. *Kubla Khan: The Emperor of Everything*. New York, NY: Viking Books for Young Readers, 2010.

May, Timothy. *The Mongol Art of War*. Yardley, PA: Westholme Publishing, 2007.

McLynn, Frank. *Genghis Khan: His Conquests, His Empire, His Legacy*. Boston, MA: Da Capo Press, 2015.

Morgan, David. *The Mongols*. Hoboken, NJ: Wiley-Blackwell, 2007.

Ropp, Paul. *China in World History.* New York, NY: Oxford University Press, 2010.

Weatherford, Jack. *Genghis Khan and the Making of the Modern World*. New York, NY: Broadway Books, 2005.

Weatherford, Jack. *The Secret History of the Mongol Queens: How the Daughters of Genghis Khan Rescued His Empire*. New York, NY: Crown, 2010.

BIBLIOGRAPHY

Asia for Educators. "Khubilai Khan in China." Asian Topics in World History, Columbia University. Retrieved November 12, 2015 (http://afe.easia.columbia.edu/mongols/china/china2.htm).

Carboni, Stefano, and Qamar Adamjee. "The Legacy of Genghis Khan." In Heilbrunn Timeline of Art History. The Metropolitan Museum of Art, October 2003 (http://www.met-museum.org/toah/hd/khan1/hd_khan1.htm).

Christiansen, Kenan. "Reconstructing Marco Polo's Journey East." *New York Times*, March 11, 2015 (http://www.nytimes.com/2015/03/15/travel/reconstructing-marco-polos-journey-east.html?_r=0).

Clare, Israel Smith. *The World's History Illuminated: Volume 5: The Middle Ages and the Reformation*. St. Louis, MO: The Western Newspaper Syndicate, 1897.

Edwards, Mike. "Lord of the Mongols." *National Geographic,* December 1996 (http://ngm.nationalgeographic.com/print/1996/12/genghis-khan/edwards-text).

Eyewitness to History. "Kublai Kahn in Battle, 1287." 2000. Retrieved December 6, 2015 (http://www.eyewitnesstohistory.com/khan.htm).

Frazier, Ian. "Invaders." *New Yorker*, April 25, 2005 (http://www.newyorker.com/magazine/2005/04/25/invaders-3).

Grace, Carrie. "Kublai Kahn: China's Favorite Barbarian." BBC News, 2012 (http://www.bbc.com/news/magazine-19850234).

Kahn, Razib. "1 in 200 Men Direct Descendants of Genghis Khan." *Discover*, August 2010 (http://blogs .discovermagazine.com/gnxp/2010/08/1-in-200-men-direct-descendants-of-genghis-khan/#.VnArT3grLIU).

Mann, John. *Kublai Kahn: The Mongol King Who Remade China*. London, England: Bantam Books, 2006.

Newark, Tim. *The Barbarians: Warriors and Wars of the Dark Ages*. Dorset, England: Blandford Press, 1985.

Polo, Marco. *The Travels of Marco Polo*. New York, NY: Harper & Brothers, 1855.

Rossabi, Morris. *Khubilai Khan: His Life and Times*. Berkeley, CA: University of California Press, 1988.

Ryall, Julian. "13th Century Mongolian Ship Kublai Kahn Sent to Invade Japan Found." *Telegraph*, July 2015 (http://www.telegraph.co.uk/news/worldnews/asia/ japan/11715158/13th-century-Mongolian-ship-Kublai-Khan-sent-to-invade-Japan-found.html).

Time. "Exploring the World of the Great Kublai Kahn." Retrieved December 10, 2015 (http://content.time.com/time/ photogallery/0,29307,2027165,00.html).

INDEX

A

Alghu, 37
Ariq, 32, 33, 35–36, 37

B

Batu, 21–23, 37
Beijing, 9, 20, 37
Berke, 37
Buddhism, 8, 15, 20, 50

C

Chabi, 50
Chagatei Khanante, 37, 52
Confucianism, 8, 15, 20

D

Dadu, 38
Dalis, 24, 25–27, 29

E

Europe, 6, 26, 43, 49

G

Genghis Khan, 6, 25, 27, 30, 33,
      37, 42, 43, 52, 53, 54
   advancements made by,
   13–14
   childhood of, 11, 13
   death of, 16
   invades China, 9, 11, 13
   religious and cultural
   tolerance, 14, 18
   unites Mongol tribes,
   9, 13

Golden Horde, 21, 37, 52
Guyuk, 21–22, 23, 33

H

Haiyun, 20, 50
Hulegu, 32, 33, 37, 40

J

Japan, invasions of, 51–52
Jins, 9, 13, 37

K

Karakorum, 30, 35
Kerait tribe, 12
Khwarazmian dynasty, 13
Kublai Khan
      advancements made
       during rule, 8, 23, 30,
      42, 47, 53
      becomes Great Khan, 7,
      32–36, 37, 42
      culture/arts and, 6, 8,
      15, 20, 30, 32, 43, 50
      birth/childhood of, 12,
      15, 16
      in China, 6–7, 20, 23,
      27–29, 30, 32, 34–35,
      37–42
      combat operations,
      25–29, 31–32, 40–42
      decline and death of,
      50–53
      family tree, 33
      as governor, 19–20, 21,

23, 29–30
helping the poor, 6, 20,
35, 42, 53
legacy of, 8, 53–54
size of empire, 6
unifying of cultures/
countries, 6, 8, 20, 39–
40, 42, 43
kurultai, 21, 31, 32

M
Mongke, 23, 24, 25, 27, 29–30,
31–32, 33
Mongolia, 9, 11, 13, 15, 16, 20,
32, 37, 38, 54
Mongols
about, 7–8, 13, 15, 18,
26, 32
decline of empire, 53
as horsemen, 9, 24, 26,
40
invasions of China,
9–11, 16, 18, 24, 25–29,
30, 31–32, 37
size of empire, 6, 11, 13,
43

O
Ogedei, 16–18, 19, 21, 23, 33

P
Persia, 32, 33, 37, 40, 49
Polo, Marco, 6, 8, 43–49, 54

R
Rustichello, 48, 49

S
Silk Road, 7, 45
Song dynasty, 23, 24, 25, 29,
30, 31–32, 39–42, 43, 50
Sorghaghtani, 12, 14–15, 16–18
19, 20, 21–22, 23, 30, 33

T
Temur, 33, 53
Tolui, 12, 16, 18, 33
Travels of Marco Polo, The, 48
trebuchets, 40

X
Xanadu, 30, 31, 37
Xiangyang, 40–41, 48
Xia Xia, 13

Y
Yangtze River, 25, 27, 32
Yuan dynasty, 20, 39, 53
Yunnan province, 25, 53

Z
Zhengding, 18
Zhenjin, 50
Zhongdu, 9, 12

ABOUT THE AUTHOR

Andrew Vietze is the author of nine books, including the best-seller *Boon Island* and the award-winning biography *Becoming Teddy Roosevelt*. He lives in Maine.

PHOTO CREDITS

Cover, p. 3 (Kublai Khan) Hulton Archive/Getty Images; cover, p. 3 (map) © iStockphoto.com/Whiteway; interior pages background image (landscape) © iStockphoto.com/joyt; p. 7 © Classic Image/Alamy Stock Photo; p. 10, 48 Heritage Images/Hulton Archive/Getty Images; p. 11 Wolfgang Kaehler/LightRocket/Getty Images; pp. 14, 22, 51 Pictures from History/Bridgeman Images; p. 17 Sean Gallagher/National Geographic Magazines/Getty Images; p. 19 Werner Forman Archive/Bridgeman Images; pp. 28, 36 Werner Forman/Hulton Fine Art Collection/Getty Images; p. 29 Imaginechina/AP Images; p. 34 Freer Gallery, Smithsonian Institution, Washington, USA/Bridgeman Images; p. 38 DEA Picture Library/De Agostini/Getty Images; p. 41 Edinburgh University Library, Scotland/With kind permission of the University of Edinburgh/Bridgeman Images; p. 44 Print Collector/Hulton Archive/Getty Images; p. 46 National Museum of Chinese History, Beijing/Ancient Art and Architecture Collection Ltd./Bridgeman Images

Designer: Matt Cauli; Editor: Meredith Day; Photo Researcher: Nicole DiMella